SUNNY SIDE UP

A Guide to Cracking Open Your Retirement Nest Egg

SUNNY SIDE UP

A Guide to Cracking Open Your Retirement Nest Egg

ROCH TRANEL & BEN PAHL

Copyright © 2015 by Roch Tranel & Ben Pahl

All rights reserved. No part of this publication may be reproduced, stored in a retrieval system, or transmitted, in any form or by any means, electronic, mechanical, photocopying, recording, or otherwise, without the prior written permission of the author.

ISBN-13: 978-1987605150
LCCN: 1987605152

For more information go to:
www.mysunnysideup.com
www.tranelfinancial.com
1509 N Milwaukee Ave.
Libertyville, IL 60048
847.680.9052
info@mysunnysideup.com

Editors: Joann Dobbie & Kim Bookless
Illustrator: Tom Kepler
Cover Design: Alan Pranke

Printed in the United States of America

CONTENTS

	Introduction	1
1	**The Perfect Egg** *Cracking open the perfect nest egg*	5
2	**Emotions** *They can be deceiving*	9
3	**Common Fears** *We all have them*	15
4	**Inflation & Taxes** *A nest egg's worst enemies*	21
5	**Time Horizon—Concept 1** *It's not what you think*	25
6	**Sequence of Returns—Concept 2** *Timing is everything*	31
7	**Dollar Cost Averaging—Concept 3** *It sounds complicated—It's not*	43
8	**The Bucket System—Our Core Strategy** *Time to crack open your nest egg!*	53
9	**Cooking the Egg** *The egg has been cracked. No pieces of shell anywhere. Now what?*	69
10	**The Next Step** *Plan to achieve your desired goals*	77
	Afterword	79

INTRODUCTION

For most baby boomers and their parents, the American Dream was a house, one or two cars, and 2.5 children. We planned to work until age 65, and then magically live our Golden Years happily ever after on Social Security and a generous company pension.

Unfortunately, the truth today is that one out of four people will run out of money during retirement. The landscape of retirement has changed significantly. The days of working at the same company for an entire career and retiring comfortably with a Social Security check and pension is no longer a reality for the majority of modern-day retirees. More and more, retirees need to rely on their own savings and investments to generate income in retirement as fewer and fewer companies offer pensions.

We are at the beginning of a huge transformation from an old economy to a new one, and are facing such a massive change that it is often hard to fathom. Modern retirees also find themselves envisioning an active and fulfilling retirement—full of traveling, spoiling grandkids, picking up a new hobby, volunteering, or starting a small business. The concept of settling down or even slowing down in retirement is quickly becoming a thing of the past as today's baby boomers transition into this exciting stage of their lives.

In this incredible era of innovative thought and new technologies that bring change and progress, we must also think and manage our retirement money just as creatively. In addition, although today's retirees have worked hard to accumulate wealth, they may not be aware of the many options for protecting and growing their money during their retirement years.

Since information on everything under the sun can be found online, you might think that you could just click on a web page or download an app and it would solve all your financial problems. That is not the case. That's why we wrote this book: to share a powerful new approach to understanding and managing your money so you can enjoy an active, fulfilling retirement.

The fact is that traveling, hobbies, and grandkids require more cash flow and income than Social Security and pensions will provide. This book focuses on how to make the best use of your nest egg once you transition from your working years to retirement. *Sunny Side Up* will shape your thinking and ultimately give you a proven strategy for how to effectively crack open your nest egg in retirement. Having the right mindset, understanding fundamental financial concepts, and working within the right strategy are the keys to making sure your retirement savings will be there to see you through the retirement you envision.

INTRODUCTION

Sunny Side Up offers an innovative, refreshing approach to generating income from retirement savings. This book explores and explains many of the common emotions and fears you may face as you manage your finances through retirement. In the next section, we will take a deep dive into three concepts that are critical, yet often misunderstood by most retirees: time horizon, sequence of returns, and dollar cost averaging. These three concepts are woven into a powerful strategy—The Bucket System—giving you a road map for how to structure your nest egg to generate consistent and reliable cash flow throughout retirement.

Finance and investments can be complicated. Your retirement income strategy doesn't have to be. *Sunny Side Up* will give you the knowledge necessary to simplify your finances and will help you live a fulfilling and enjoyable retirement.

When you are planning for retirement and eventually retire, you are faced with cracking open your nest egg. You have only one chance to get it right. This essential handbook will give you the insight and tools necessary for that success.

Chapter 1

THE PERFECT EGG

Cracking open the perfect nest egg

Think back to when you first learned to crack an egg. Were you baking cookies with your grandma? Were you making breakfast with your dad? Or were you cooking meals for yourself when you moved into your own apartment? Whatever the case, reach into your memory bank and visualize the picture of you learning how to crack an egg.

Like most people, the first few times you cracked an egg, it did not go according to plan. If you tap too soft, it does not crack. If you tap too hard, the egg splatters all over. Then, the next step challenges us to figure out how to pull the egg apart without pieces of shell falling into our recipe. We can all relate to using a spoon to scoop out small pieces of shell that have fallen into our frying pan or bowl.

The nice thing about learning to crack eggs is there are plenty of eggs to practice with. If you make a mistake, you simply reach into the carton and grab another egg. With each attempt, you get better and better. And before you know it, you are a pro!

When it comes to retirement planning, there is a type of egg that often steals the show. It's called the nest egg. The nest egg is the money you have set aside for your retirement. First, it's the money you plan to utilize for income, and second, it's the money you want for those various bucket list items you didn't have time for during your working years. Your nest egg, and how it is managed, will have a significant impact on how you spend your golden years.

When the decision is made to retire and you are now faced with "cracking open" your retirement nest egg, there is only one chance to do it right. There are no extra eggs in the carton to practice with.

The decisions you make with your nest egg will affect the way you live your life in retirement. How you invest it, draw income from it, structure it, and think about it will play a major role in the overall outcome of your finances in retirement.

In this book, you will learn important retirement planning concepts and strategies that will change the way you think about money, especially retirement money. Our mission is to educate you about the pivotal things you need to know to help ensure a full and prosperous retirement. Ultimately, this book will show you how to crack open the perfect nest egg—Sunny Side Up.

A Look At What's Ahead . . .

You are about to embark on a guided tour of our time-tested core retirement strategy.[1] But first, it's critical to

---

[1] All investing involves risk, including the potential loss of principal, and there can be no guarantee that any investment strategy will be successful.

lay a solid foundation. There are several vital thoughts and concepts you should learn to ensure you will truly grasp just how powerful this core strategy is for you and your retirement plan. These concepts serve as the building blocks for the strategy behind the perfect nest egg. In order to understand **our strategy**, you first need to understand the concepts.

We will begin with a brief discussion about *emotions*. Money plays a significant role in your life and, naturally, there is a lot of emotion tied to it. Because there are many different fears and concerns retirees face and overcome throughout retirement, these emotions are discussed separately. Then, your nest egg's worst enemies, *taxes* and *inflation*, will be explored. And last, there are three critical concepts you should become familiar with: time horizon, sequence of returns, and dollar cost averaging. For those of you who feel you have a deep understanding of these concepts, they will be explained much differently than you have heard them explained before.

Once you have a suitable grasp of these concepts, attention will shift toward unveiling our core retirement planning strategy known as The Bucket System. Then, you will be given a detailed analysis of types of investments, and when to use them, with this strategy.

Gaining a strong understanding of the material in this book is absolutely vital to cracking open the perfect nest egg. To help you in this endeavor, several videos are designed to walk you through all the concepts and the core strategy. These videos can be found at www.mysunnysideup.com.

Overall, this book should have a significant impact on how you manage your retirement money. It will serve as a source of clarity and confidence when it comes to thinking about your nest egg. Your retirement nest egg should generate a predictable and sustainable income stream for you and your family for many years to come.

Chapter 2
EMOTIONS

*They can be deceiving.
When it comes to investments, what your
emotions tell you to do is often the exact
opposite of what you should do.*

When asked to name the four things most important to them, most people will give the same answers, in varying order. These four things are health, family, money, and faith. Strong emotions are tied to these because a lot of emotional value is invested in each one.

Money, and the role it plays in your life, is very important. Fundamentally, it's how you put food on the table, a roof over your head, clothes on your back, and provide for your family. We earn it, save it, spend it, donate it, invest it, borrow it, and lend it. A substantial amount of emotion is tied to money because it represents so many different aspects of our lives. Money gives us peace of mind and a sense of security. It also gives us a sense of freedom that in turn awards us options. This is what retirement is. It's freedom to do the things we want to do when we want to do them.

Most people agree money does not buy happiness. Very few of us live our lives in a constant quest for money.

However, it is likely none of us would turn down money if we were offered more. For example, when is the last time you refused a raise from your employer?

Money is often a major determining factor in many of the decisions we make throughout our lives. As a result, the emotional power of money is very strong.

Another constant that tends to hold true revolves around the emotions someone feels when he or she either make or lose money. For many people, the pain of losing money is twice as great as the joy of gaining the same amount. The emotional pain you feel if you lose $10,000 can be twice as painful as the joy of earning $10,000.

This simple observation is a significant part of the puzzle. Financial planning is more than managing money. It is equally important to manage emotions.

Emotions, when channeled improperly, can lead to irrational decisions. They will often cause you to make the wrong decision with your money at the wrong time. When it comes to investments, what your emotions *tell* you to do is often the exact opposite of what you *should* do.

Mary is a 49-year-old buyer for a large retailer in Chicago. She is a great saver and knows the importance of setting money aside for retirement. In July 2009, she contributed the maximum amount to her employer sponsored 401(k) plan and also contributed the maximum to her Roth IRA.

In a conversation with her brother about retirement planning, she told him she had 80% of the money in her 401(k) parked in the stable value money market fund.

He was genuinely surprised and asked why someone as young as she had so much of her 401(k) invested in a low-yielding money market account.

She answered by explaining it had not always been in the money market. In fact, she moved it to the money market fund in March, just a few months before.

In reference to the 2008–2009 financial crash, March 2009 happened to be the month the markets reached their lowest levels. Mary commented to her brother she held strong during Fall 2008, staying invested through everything that was happening. In March, when the markets fell dramatically again, she decided she'd had enough. She sold the majority of her nest egg and put the money into her money market account. She could not tolerate any more downward movement in her 401(k).

Mary's reaction to the downward pressure the markets faced in March of 2009 is quite common. She simply got tired of seeing her account fall in value. It was very frustrating and frightening for Mary. Her emotions won. Her emotions told her to sell.

Thankfully, Mary got back on the right track with her investment allocation. She elected to move money from her money market to her previous asset allocation little by little until all the money was invested again. By moving 10% per month for the next ten months, she utilized dollar cost averaging. This is a concept you will read more about later in this book.

Warren Buffet has a famous saying: Be fearful when others are greedy and greedy when others are fearful.

Think back to the dot-com bubble burst in the early 2000s. Internet stocks were very hot. Dot-com companies were trading at excessively high valuations because of the intense demand to own these stocks. When there is a high demand for something, prices of that item will usually rise. Dot-com stocks were soaring and no one wanted to miss out on the great returns. Everyone wanted a piece of the action. As a result, stock prices became ridiculously overvalued, momentum was impossible to sustain, and the prices crashed to more reasonable levels.

The housing market followed a similar path in 2007 and 2008. Interest rates were very low after the recession that followed the dot-com bubble burst. With low rates, borrowing money was cheap. Cheap money, coupled with reduced mortgage lending standards, created excessive demand for real estate. With this increase in demand, prices started to soar.

During 2006 and 2007, it seemed like every other show on television was some sort of "Flip This House" program. People were buying second homes and other investment properties with the idea of "making a killing." The housing market soon became another dot-com bubble. It crashed when ridiculously high valuations could no longer be supported.

With both the dot-com bubble and the housing bubble, valuations were pushed too high because so many people wanted to get in on the action by buying stocks and real estate. They were chasing returns. They were greedy. Remember the quote from Warren Buffet: Be fearful when others are greedy. The bubble bursts when others are greedy. The emotional desire to chase returns, to flock where others are making money (thinking it is the safe and sure bet), often gets you into trouble as an investor.

Let's look at the other half of Warren Buffet's quote: Be greedy when others are fearful. If you can develop the discipline to invest in this manner then, as an investor, you have officially arrived. It is easier said than done, because it strongly goes against the emotions and instincts you feel. Remember, the emotional desire to avoid loss can be twice as strong as the desire to achieve gain.

Financial stocks experienced significant losses during the 2008 market crash. Several of the world's largest financial institutions went bankrupt or were forced to merge with stronger, slightly more stable institutions to survive. Why did financial stock prices fall so significantly? They fell because there was very low demand for owning these stocks. Where excessive demand drove prices very high during the dot-com and real estate bubble, excessive supply (i.e., everyone wanted to sell) caused prices to sharply decline in the financial sector.

Enter Berkshire Hathaway (Warren Buffet's company). From 2007–2011, Berkshire Hathaway purchased over 181 million shares of Wells Fargo stock. Notice this is NOT dollars. It's 181 million *shares*. Those shares represented over $5 billion of Wells Fargo stock purchased over the five-year stretch. A large portion of shares were purchased during the depths of the financial crash. Warren Buffet stepped up to the plate when no one else wanted to touch these stocks. When everyone else wanted out, he got in. He was able to separate himself from the emotional human instinct to avoid buying into a company like Wells Fargo during the depths of the recession. He used rational thought and analysis, rather than emotion, to realize Wells Fargo was oversold. It was excessively cheap and undervalued. This is exactly what you are looking for when it comes to a great investment. Other people's fear drove the price down. So, he became greedy and bought. In early 2009, Wells Fargo was trading under $10 per share. In 2014, it is trading at over $50 per share. This represents more than a 500% increase in a little over five years.

Emotions and money go hand in hand. It is difficult for most people to separate emotions from their investments. As we proceed through this book, you will learn practical strategies to help you manage your emotions as you make vital decisions about your retirement nest egg.

Chapter 3

COMMON FEARS

*We all have them.
Sometimes, people are very excited about
the idea of retirement but, underneath, they may
have some serious fears or concerns about the
practicality of actually retiring.*

When cracking eggs, you may fear getting an eggshell in your recipe or breaking the egg too hard and watching part of the egg spill down the outside of the bowl and onto the counter. With retirement planning, mistakes come in a far different variety and the stakes are much higher. It's important to create a predictable and sustainable income stream that will allow you to maintain your desired lifestyle for as long as you live. The largest fear for many is running out of money.

Maxine turned 66 years old and had just reached her "full retirement age," according to her social security statement. Maxine would like to retire but does not know if she should. She is debt free and lives a comfortable lifestyle. Maintaining the house, property taxes, grandkids, monthly bills, and her annual vacation are all paid for with the income she earns at her job. She started actively saving for retirement when she was 40 years old, yet admittedly wishes she started saving sooner. Since 40, Maxine has been a good saver and has about $450,000 in her nest egg. She is willing and able to work longer, but does not necessarily want to. Maxine knows her social security check will not be enough to support her desired lifestyle in retirement. And by not working, she fears she will have too much free time to spend too much extra money, putting additional strain on her savings and causing her to someday run out of money. She is torn between wanting to retire and wondering if she can or *should* retire.

As we edge closer and closer to retirement and the dream becomes a reality, this type of fear is very common. We want to make sure we are doing the right thing. Fears like those Maxine is facing can generally be consolidated into three overall themes:

1) Will I run out of money?
2) Am I maximizing my potential?
3) If I'm worried about my finances, how can I enjoy my retirement?

Will I Run Out of Money?

The fear of running out of money is a simple fear to understand. In retirement, what you have is what you have. For the most part, you are not adding additional money to a 401(k) or an IRA. You need money to maintain your lifestyle for as long as you live. You don't want to have to go back to work to earn extra money if you run out. Naturally, the fear of running out of money is a top concern for retirees.

Am I Maximizing My Potential?

The idea of maximizing your potential has a lot to do with enjoying a full and well- rounded retirement. Most of us have a vision of what we want our retirement to look like. It would be a shame to work for 30, 40, or 50 years, set money aside for retirement along the way, finally retire, and not realize the full potential of your retirement nest egg.

Because the fear of running out of money is so enormous, some people are actually scared to spend their retirement money. In a way, they need permission to use and enjoy this money.

If I'm Worried About My Finances, How Can I Enjoy My Retirement?

This particular fear is quite interesting and wasn't a real source of concern for most retirees until the 2008 recession. During this time, financial news became front-page news. Our economy, stock market, national debt, and unemployment were in the forefront of most of our minds. Naturally, retirees found themselves worried about their nest egg. They felt so anxious about their money that it caused them to stop enjoying their retirement. Ideally, you want to be worry free when it comes to your money.

The fear of not being worry free is troublesome for a lot of people.

LaMont is a client of our firm. We have a long-running conversation with LaMont. It is probably better described as a long-running joke. LaMont finds as much humor in the joke as we do. It seems like every time we call LaMont, especially when we call him in the morning, we will always hear CNBC (the money channel) in the background. LaMont is glued to the television everyday, wondering and worrying about what the financial markets are doing. LaMont has been retired since 2006 and we keep telling him he will never look back on life wishing he watched more financial news. We tell him life is for living—he needs to get out there and live it. He needs to enjoy retirement and let us worry about what the markets are doing. We tell him that watching the news will not change the outcome. We always have a laugh or two about his choice of programming because he knows we're right, but he can't help himself. When LaMont sees our phone number come across his caller ID, he doesn't even say hello when he answers. He simply says "You caught me again," and we know what he's talking about.

LaMont is a great guy and certainly lives an active and fulfilling retirement. However, you can bet he has CNBC on every minute he is in his house. At his core, LaMont is watching the markets because he is nervous about how the markets will affect his nest egg—the nest egg he relies on to support his lifestyle in retirement. LaMont's fear is a common fear many retirees need to face and overcome.

In structuring your retirement plan, it's crucial to understand these three common fears. It's important to have clarity and confidence about your future so the fears are a non-issue. You want peace of mind in your retirement years. As you continue your journey through this book, you will learn many different concepts to help shape your thinking about retirement planning. Ultimately, your goal is to have a great strategy designed to combat all the different emotions and fears surrounding your retirement nest egg.

Chapter 4
INFLATION & TAXES

A nest egg's worst enemies

Time can do some pretty amazing things. As time passes, our world is constantly changing. We do not notice many of these changes on a day-to-day, month-to-month, or even year-to-year basis. The changes are so subtle, but in the long run, can be so massive.

Stand in front of a mirror today and take a good look at yourself. Stand in front of a mirror tomorrow and take another good look at yourself. Chances are, you will see yourself and tell yourself you look exactly the same. Do it again the next day and you will once again see no differences compared to the day before. In fact, if you look in the mirror everyday for ten years, your mind may never notice a difference. However, look at a picture of yourself from ten years ago and everything will look different. The changes from day to day and month to month are too subtle for our brains to notice. But, over a long period of time, the changes can be significant.

From one day to the next, we don't notice the grass in our yard getting higher. But after about a week, it's time to mow the lawn again. We also don't notice our hair getting longer. But after a couple of weeks, it is time to get our hair cut again.

Inflation works in a very similar way. We don't always feel it and we don't always see it. But it is there. Inflation, put simply, is the sustained rise in the cost of living over time. The cost of things like food, energy, gasoline, and other goods and services tend to increase over time. This causes us to need more and more income every year to keep pace with the rising cost of living—to keep pace with inflation.

Inflation is a critical component in your retirement plan. A well-constructed retirement plan will include an inflation factor to ensure the nest egg sustains a reasonable amount of inflation through the duration of retirement.

Over a 20-year period, just a 3% inflation rate will cause the cost of living to increase by 80%. This means if you need a $50,000 income when you are 60 years old, you will need a $90,305 income when you are 80 to maintain the same lifestyle. This is a very significant increase when looking at a 20-year period. On top of that, I'm sure you will agree, we all hope our retirement lasts much longer than 20 years. This will ultimately compound the impact of inflation even more.

Taxes

Besides inflation, taxes are another serious component that should be built into your retirement plan. Both income tax and capital gains tax can significantly erode the buying power of your nest egg over the long run.

Imagine you need $40,000 to buy a car and a traditional IRA is your main source of funds in retirement. Assume you pay 25% in local and federal taxes. You would actually need to withdraw $53,333 to net $40,000 after taxes!

Forget big-ticket items like cars and vacation. Let's simply examine how taxes can affect monthly income. Assuming 25% total taxes once again, and also assuming you need $2,500 per month NET income from your IRA, you will actually need to withdraw $3,333 GROSS income every month to net the $2,500 income you are looking for. Every month, you need $833 for taxes. Over the course of a year, you need $10,000 for taxes!

What you saved for your retirement is not necessarily what you have to spend on yourself and your family in retirement. Taxes will certainly cut into your savings as you draw income. And, inflation will cause the amount you need to withdraw every year to increase. This, in turn, will cause you to pay more in taxes.

You can see why we refer to taxes and inflation as a nest egg's worst enemies. The good news is, with proper planning and execution, you can account for inflation and taxes without taking a pay cut or adjusting your lifestyle down the road.

Chapter 5

TIME HORIZON CONCEPT 1

It's not what you think
The time horizon for your retirement money
is not the day you are going to retire—it's the
day you are going to pass away.

With eggs, the time horizon is easy to figure out. It's as simple as reading the expiration date on the side of the carton. When it comes to retirement planning, it is not quite that straightforward.

The more time you have until you need to use the funds you are investing, the more aggressive you can afford to be. As you draw closer to the time you need the funds, you should become more conservative.

The logic behind this concept stems from the fact that having a long period of time on your side affords you the ability to tolerate a higher degree of fluctuation within your account in exchange for a greater potential long-run return. If your account decreases in value, you have time on your side—time for it to recover in value and time to add more funds to the account at reduced prices.

If your time horizon is short and you end up with a decrease in account value, it can be difficult to recover. You may not have enough time to wait out the recovery. Ultimately, you could end up cashing in your investment at a loss if you get too aggressive with a short time horizon.

College planning is a good example. When a child is born, there is roughly an 18-year time horizon to save for college. If the parents have funds to start a college savings plan early, they can afford to be aggressive with their investment choices within this plan. An 18-year time horizon is plenty of time to tolerate some ups and downs in exchange for a higher return. As the child reaches middle school, the parents should change to a more balanced allocation. When the child reaches 10th or 11th grade, the child's college account should move to a more conservative allocation. It's important to avoid any major losses within the account right before the parents intend to use the funds for college.

As your time horizon shortens, your investment allocation should become more conservative.

However, when it comes to retirement planning, the concept of time horizon becomes much more complex. It's critical to think of time horizon differently when putting together a retirement plan.

If you are 60 years old and plan to retire when you are 65, what is the time horizon for your retirement money? Most people will answer "five years." The time horizon for your retirement money is not the day you are going to retire—it's the day you are going to pass away. That's how long you need your money to last.

The problem with this concept is no one knows how long he or she will live. With college planning, time horizon can be measured with a high degree of clarity. Generally, the first withdrawal is made from the college account when a child turns 18 and the last withdrawal is taken when the child is 22 years old. The time horizon for college planning is clearly defined and, therefore, easy to plan for.

Retirement planning is completely different. You don't know how long you are going to live, so you don't know how long your money needs to last.

It's important to think of retirement planning as a series of staggered time horizons, not one lump sum of money all with the same time horizon.

Assume again you are 60 years old and intend to retire when you are 65. Yes, some of the money you have in your nest egg will be used when you are 65. But, some will be needed when you are 70, 75, 80, 85, 90, etc. A large portion of your nest egg won't be used until 10, 20, or 30 years down the road. It certainly does not make sense to invest your five-year money the same way you invest your 20-year money.

Many people make the mistake of mentally lumping their retirement money together and investing it all the same way. It is very common for people in their mid-fifties and early sixties to invest their funds very conservatively because they view themselves as having a short time horizon for their retirement money. In fact, portions of the money they have in their retirement nest egg won't be touched for 20–30 years.

If you were 20 years younger, would you worry about how your retirement money is invested? Most people would say, "No, there is no need to worry. Retirement is still 20 years away."

A 60- or 70-year-old should realize some of the money set aside for retirement won't be needed for another 20 years. This money can be invested the same way it was invested 20 years ago. It should be positioned for long-term growth, knowing you have plenty of time on your side.

When you segment your retirement nest egg into different accounts and assign each account a different time horizon, it makes the ups and downs of the investments much more tolerable. Your short-term accounts are very conservative. They will modestly fluctuate as the time horizon approaches, so you can feel secure and confident. Meanwhile, your long-term accounts are more aggressive. They will fluctuate more along the way. This is your long-term money and it is supposed to have a higher degree of fluctuation in an effort to gain a larger potential return over time.

This concept is extremely vital for today's retiree to grasp. Life expectancies are longer and the cost of living continues to increase. In order to combat this, it's important for your nest egg to be invested in a way that allows for substantial growth over time with a portion of your money (long-term accounts) balanced with safety and security (short-term accounts).

If you are too conservative with too much of your money too early, it could cause inflation and taxes to eat away at your nest egg too soon. This leaves you with a much smaller nest egg than you intended for your retirement years.

Retirement will hopefully be a *long* and *enjoyable* journey for you. Invest accordingly.

Chapter 6

SEQUENCE OF RETURNS CONCEPT 2

Timing is everything
Two people retire at the same time with the same amount of money and start withdrawing the same income stream. Their portfolios average the same return over the course of their retirement. One runs out of money in the middle of retirement and the other has millions of dollars to pass on to family members. How can this be?

When it comes to eggs, we really don't know the exact timing of the chicken and egg scenario. You know, the age-old question: Which came first—the chicken or the egg? You can't have a chicken without an egg for it to hatch from and you can't have an egg without a chicken to lay it. Thankfully, we don't need to solve this mystery. Nevertheless, we do need to solve and overcome something we call *timing risk*. It is absolutely vital to address this risk when constructing your retirement plan. If you are on the wrong side, it can make or break your retirement. Ultimately, if you become a victim of bad timing, it can cause you to run out of money.

"Sequence of returns" is an eye opener for anyone exposed to this concept for the first time. Once you understand how and why it works, it will completely change the way you think about investing your nest egg, both before and during retirement.

Think of your retirement planning lifecycle in two different time periods:

1) Accumulation Phase
2) Distribution Phase

The accumulation phase represents the time saving, or accumulating, money for retirement. This phase is building the nest egg. The distribution phase represents the time you start drawing income from your nest egg. Distributing funds to yourself helps supplement your other income sources in retirement.

This concept is explained further in the following illustrations.

The chart at the top of the next page shows an example of two investors, Alan and Brian. They both invested $100,000 at age 40 and left the money untouched for 25 years. Over that 25-year period, they earned various rates of return. Some years produced very positive returns and some years produced very negative returns. This illustration does not represent any particular investment. It is simply a sequence of random returns designed to illustrate this very important retirement planning concept.

Accumulation Phase
Starting Value of Portfolios: $100,000

Age	Annual Return	Alan's Portfolio Year-End Value	Annual Return	Brian's Portfolio Year-End Value
41	17%	$117,000		
42	18%	$138,060		
43	26%	$173,956		
44	-4%	$166,997		
45	15%	$192,047		
46	17%	$224,695		
47	23%	$276,375		
48	18%	$326,122		
49	-3%	$316,339		
50	19%	$376,443		
51	31%	$493,140		
52	5%	$517,797		
53	-9%	$471,196		
54	10%	$518,315		
55	19%	$616,795		
56	28%	$789,498		
57	-7%	$734,233		
58	6%	$778,287		
59	14%	$887,247		
60	3%	$913,864		
61	12%	$1,023,528		
62	26%	$1,289,645		
63	-28%	$928,544		
64	-18%	$761,406		
65	-13%	$662,424		

As you can see, Alan's first three years of returns are very good and the last three years are very bad. Over this 25-year time frame, Alan's $100,000 grows to $662,424.

Brian's returns are the exact same returns Alan received except they are completely reversed. The negative returns occur in the earlier years and the positive returns occur in the later years. Given Brian's complete reversal of rates of return, how do you think the end result changes? Is the end result higher or lower than $662,424?

Believe it or not, the end result is exactly the same! The explanation is shown in the chart on the next page.

SEQUENCE OF RETURNS CONCEPT 2

Accumulation Phase
Starting Value of Portfolios: $100,000

Age	Annual Return	Alan's Portfolio Year-End Value	Annual Return	Brian's Portfolio Year-End Value
41	17%	$117,000	-13%	$87,000
42	18%	$138,060	-18%	$71,340
43	26%	$173,956	-28%	$51,365
44	-4%	$166,997	26%	$64,720
45	15%	$192,047	12%	$72,486
46	17%	$224,695	3%	$74,661
47	23%	$276,375	14%	$85,113
48	18%	$326,122	6%	$90,220
49	-3%	$316,339	-7%	$83,904
50	19%	$376,443	28%	$107,398
51	31%	$493,140	19%	$127,803
52	5%	$517,797	10%	$140,584
53	-9%	$471,196	-9%	$127,931
54	10%	$518,315	5%	$134,328
55	19%	$616,795	31%	$175,969
56	28%	$789,498	19%	$209,403
57	-7%	$734,233	-3%	$203,121
58	6%	$778,287	18%	$239,683
59	14%	$887,247	23%	$294,810
60	3%	$913,864	17%	$344,928
61	12%	$1,023,528	15%	$396,667
62	26%	$1,289,645	-4%	$380,800
63	-28%	$928,544	26%	$479,809
64	-18%	$761,406	18%	$566,174
65	-13%	$662,424	17%	$662,424
	9%	$662,424	9%	$662,424

Here's why this works:

3 x 2 x 1 = 6
1 x 2 x 3 = 6
2 x 3 x 1 = 6
1 x 3 x 2 = 6

No matter what order you multiply these numbers, the answer is *always* six and the average is *always* two.

When working with the sequence of returns illustrated above, place the return numbers in any order and the end result is the same because the *average* is the same. If you average the same return over the same period of time you will obtain the same result, regardless of the sequence in which the returns are earned!

Understanding this concept is important in the accumulation phase because it helps keep emotions in check. It is very easy to become frustrated with your investments when your accounts are losing value. It is very easy to hit the sell button when things are not going according to plan. However, as long as you are properly diversified and investing according to the proper time horizon, you should stay the course. The sequence of returns does not matter. What matters is the average return.

There will be years when you earn great returns on your money and there will be years when your account goes down in value. The only thing that's important is the average return over the period of time you wish to invest. The individual years, both good and bad, no matter when they happen or what order they come in, don't really make a difference when accumulating money for retirement. The end result is the same because the average is the same.

When you think about the sequence of returns in this manner, it makes it much easier to stay the course through both the good and the bad times. In your more aggressive accounts, you invest funds with the intention of earning a higher return over time in exchange for a higher degree of volatility along the way. Volatility, in a way, is actually part of the plan. After all, without volatility, everyone would be very aggressive with all their money all the time. Even with volatility as part of the plan, it can be a bit nerve-racking watching your more aggressive accounts fluctuate. That's when you need to lean on your knowledge of sequence of returns. You are more aggressive with part of your money because you are seeking a higher long-run *average* return. When you focus on the long-run *average*, the individual annual returns and the order they come will no longer matter to you.

Let's take the concept one step forward. Go back to our examples of Alan and Brian. They are now 65 years old and both have $662,424 in their nest egg. As mentioned earlier, they arrived at that number in different ways. However, since they averaged the same return over the same period of time, they both ended up in the same place at age 65.

Transitioning from the Accumulation Phase to the Distribution Phase

Alan and Brian are now ready to retire and enter into the distribution phase of their financial life cycle. To supplement their other income sources, they start withdrawing money from their nest egg.

We will assume they are both going to withdraw a 5% income stream from their starting value and increase the withdrawal every year by 3% to keep pace with inflation. We will also assume they will each live until age 90 (25 years from age 65) and will earn the exact same returns in their distribution phase as they did in the accumulation phase.

Take a look at the following illustration. The returns Alan received from age 65 to 90 are the exact same returns he received from age 40 to 65. This is also true for Brian. Look closer at the illustration and you will notice that Alan, at age 90, has over $2,400,000 and Brian, at age 79, ran out of money!

SEQUENCE OF RETURNS CONCEPT 2

Distribution Phase
Starting Value of Portfolios: $662,424

Age	Annual Return	Alan's Portfolio Year-End Value	Annual Return	Brian's Portfolio Year-End Value
66	17%	$741,914	-13%	$543,187
67	18%	$841,344	-18%	$411,299
68	26%	$1,024,956	-28%	$260,997
69	-4%	$947,765	26%	$292,664
70	15%	$1,052,651	12%	$290,505
71	17%	$1,193,206	3%	$260,824
72	23%	$1,428,095	14%	$257,791
73	18%	$1,644,417	6%	$232,523
74	-3%	$1,553,127	-7%	$174,290
75	19%	$1,805,006	28%	$179,875
76	31%	$2,320,045	19%	$169,539
77	5%	$2,390,200	10%	$140,646
78	-9%	$2,127,859	-9%	$80,765
79	10%	$2,292,006	5%	$36,163
80	19%	$2,677,388	31%	$0
81	28%	$3,375,455	19%	$0
82	-7%	$3,086,023	-3%	$0
83	6%	$3,216,441	18%	$0
84	14%	$3,610,356	23%	$0
85	3%	$3,660,588	17%	$0
86	12%	$4,040,038	15%	$0
87	26%	$5,028,833	-4%	$0
88	-28%	$3,557,296	26%	$0
89	-18%	$2,851,615	18%	$0
90	-13%	$2,413,577	17%	$0
	9%	$2,413,577	9%	$0

How can this be? Both averaged 9% on their money, just like they did in the accumulation phase. But they ended up with drastically different results.

The drastic difference between Alan and Brian's retirement incomes can be explained because Alan started his retirement with three great years and Brian started with three bad years. It is important to remember both Alan and Brian are withdrawing 5% per year, adjusted for inflation every year. This means in year one, not only is Brian withdrawing 5% for income purposes, but his account is also decreasing in value by 13%, causing further depletion of his account. In year two, it is a similar story. Brian is withdrawing money for income purposes AND his account lost value again. When this happens, Brian can never catch up to where he needs to be. The damage is done. If he maintains his current withdrawal rate, he will run out of money at age 79.

Alan, on the other hand, earned great returns his first few years of retirement. In fact, he was earning more than the 5% withdrawal rate he was taking. This allowed the account to continue to grow. Alan, because he got off to a great start, has a substantially different account balance than Brian just five years into retirement.

As you can see from this illustration, the returns realized in the early years of the distribution phase can make or break your retirement. Brian will certainly need to reduce the income stream from his nest egg in an effort to preserve his account for later in life.

In the accumulation phase, the sequence of return

does not matter. What is important is the average return. In the distribution phase, timing is everything. The sequence of returns will make or break your entire outcome. Even though Alan and Brian were invested in portfolios that averaged 9% over their 25-year retirement, they ended up with very different outcomes because the return came in a different sequence.

The core lesson to be learned from this concept is the fact that **in retirement you should be more concerned with minimizing the volatility of your investments than maximizing the return on your investments.** This is particularly true when taking income from your nest egg. In essence, you should be willing to accept a 6% relatively stable return over a 9% volatile return any day. The return will not make or break you. Volatility will.

At this point you may be thinking we are contradicting ourselves. After all, you just read the chapter on time horizon where we drive home the fact retirees need to invest according to their life expectancy. Retirees should allow themselves to be moderately aggressive because retirement is a long journey and it is important to be able to combat both rising taxes and inflation through the journey. Even so, with a moderately aggressive allocation, you can expect a fair amount of volatility. And this is the exact thing we are telling you to avoid in this chapter. We are not contradicting ourselves. You can actually do *both*. We will show you how as we progress through later chapters. For now, we just want you to have a clear understanding of the sequence of returns concept.

No one has a crystal ball. No one knows how their investments will perform when they retire. And no one knows if they will retire into a bull market or a bear market. This is not a variable you can leave to chance. It is much too important. The risk needs to be managed.

Note: Each sequence of returns has an average compounded annualized return of 9% over 25 years. The returns are hypothetical and for illustration purposes only. The portfolios in the accumulation phase assume a starting value of $100,000 invested at year end of the investor's age 40 and do not have any withdrawals. The portfolios in the distribution phase assume a starting value of $662,424 at age 65 and have withdrawals based on 5% of the initial value for the first year and then increased by 3% annually for inflation. Withdrawals are taken at the end of each year.

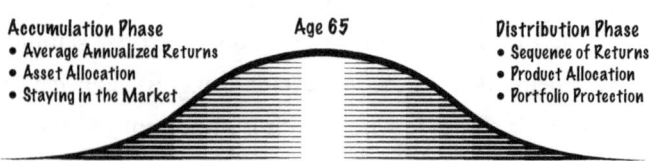

In the accumulation phase, sequence of return does not matter

In the distribution phase, sequence of return can have a dramatic impact on the end result

Chapter 7

DOLLAR COST AVERAGING CONCEPT 3

*It sounds complicated—it's not.
This concept is vital to your retirement plan. It is not always about finding consistent and steady performers. Sometimes, especially when you are regularly adding money to an account, you will want some volatility.*

If you are reading this book, chances are you have some sort of retirement account in place for yourself. It could be a Roth IRA, Traditional IRA, 401(k), 403(b), SEP, SIMPLE, or any combination thereof. Most people, when faced with the decision to choose investment options for their contributions, will first look at the historical performance of the various fund options. For employer-based plans, the plan sponsor will often hand out literature outlining the one-, three-, five-, and ten-year performance numbers. For your personal IRA account, you likely did some research on the best performing mutual funds available at the time. It's human nature. Everyone wants the highest return they can earn on their money. So, it makes sense to seek out the mutual funds with the best track record.

Many people contribute regularly to a retirement plan of some sort. If you have an employer-based plan such as a 401(k) or a 403(b), you likely contribute every pay period. If you have a Roth or Traditional IRA, you probably make contributions to it every month, or at least once per year at tax time. No matter the type of retirement plan, chances are you add money to it on a regular basis.

Let's imagine you started a new job. You plan to deduct 10% from each paycheck to contribute into your new 401(k) plan. The next step is to decide which investment options to choose.

While researching the available funds, you narrow your choice to two. For the sake of this illustration, we call these the Triangle Fund and the Square Fund. You find a graph that shows the historical performance of these investment options.

Both investments start at a $10 share price. The Square Fund increases by 50 cents every pay period, like clockwork. It never has a down stretch. After the 23rd pay period, the $10 initial share price is worth $21.50.

The Triangle Fund, on the other hand, started at the same $10 share price but did not fare nearly as well. It fell below the initial $10 price right out of the starting gate. At one point, it fell all the way to $4 per share. It fluctuated up and down, never getting back to the original $10 until the very end. It started at $10 and ended at $10.

The following illustration shows the historical performance of the two funds. Which one would you choose to contribute to every pay period within your 401(k)?

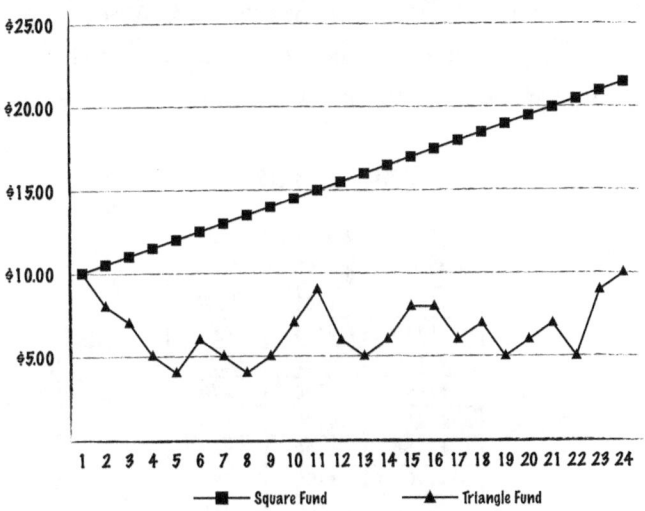

If you are like most people, you would select the Square Fund. However, the Triangle Fund makes you more money! Dollar cost averaging makes this possible. Let's first examine the chart that proves the Triangle Fund makes more money than the Square Fund over these 23 investment periods. Keep in mind, you are adding money to each fund every pay period via your 401(k) contribution.

Square Fund

Share Price	Amount Invested	# of Shares
$10.00	$100	10.00
$10.50	$100	9.52
$11.00	$100	9.09
$11.50	$100	8.70
$12.00	$100	8.33
$12.50	$100	8.00
$13.00	$100	7.69
$13.50	$100	7.41
$14.00	$100	7.14
$14.50	$100	6.90
$15.00	$100	6.67
$15.50	$100	6.45
$16.00	$100	6.25
$16.50	$100	6.06
$17.00	$100	5.88
$17.50	$100	5.71
$18.00	$100	5.56
$18.50	$100	5.41
$19.00	$100	5.26
$19.50	$100	5.13
$20.00	$100	5.00
$20.50	$100	4.88
$21.00	$100	4.76
$21.50	$100	4.65
TOTALS	**$2,400**	**160.45**

Value: $3,450

We will assume your 401(k) contribution is $100 per pay period. Your initial investment into the Square Fund, with a starting price of $10 per share, allows you to buy ten shares. Every period, the share price increases by 50 cents, becoming more expensive. Naturally, your $100 investment will buy fewer shares every time. For example, when the Square Fund is valued at $16 per share, your $100 investment will buy 6.25 shares. When it is $20 per share, your $100 investment will buy only 5 shares. When all is said and done, you will have 160.45 shares of the Square Fund with a share price of $21.50 per share, giving you an ending value of $3,450.

The Triangle Fund also starts at $10 per share. In period one, your $100 investment will buy ten shares. This is the same number of Square Fund shares you were able to buy. This is where the similarities between the two funds stop.

The Triangle Fund quickly falls to $7 per share. With your $100 contribution, you are able to purchase 14.29 shares. When it eventually falls to $4 per share, you can purchase 25 shares. The cheaper the price, the more shares you can buy with your $100 investment. (See chart next page.)

Triangle Fund

Share Price	Amount Invested	# of Shares
$10.00	$100	10.00
$8.00	$100	12.50
$7.00	$100	14.29
$5.00	$100	20.00
$4.00	$100	25.00
$6.00	$100	16.67
$5.00	$100	20.00
$4.00	$100	25.00
$5.00	$100	20.00
$7.00	$100	14.29
$9.00	$100	11.11
$6.00	$100	16.67
$5.00	$100	20.00
$6.00	$100	16.67
$8.00	$100	12.50
$8.00	$100	12.50
$6.00	$100	16.67
$7.00	$100	14.29
$5.00	$100	20.00
$6.00	$100	16.67
$7.00	$100	14.29
$5.00	$100	20.00
$9.00	$100	11.11
$10.00	$100	10.00
TOTALS	**$2,400**	**390.20**

Value: $3,902

DOLLAR COST AVERAGING CONCEPT 3

After 23 pay periods, you have accumulated 390.20 shares of the Triangle Fund. Those shares are worth the original starting value of $10 per share, giving you a total value of $3,902. This is $452 more than the Square Fund ending value, and the Square Fund grew all the way to $21.50 per share!

What makes this possible?

Think back to the $4 share price for the Triangle Fund. When you invested $100 at this price, you bought 25 shares. Eventually, those 25 shares were worth $10 per share for a total of $250. The result is a $150 profit. The volatility of the Triangle Fund worked to your advantage. It gave you the ability to accumulate more shares during the bad times and gave your overall return a boost.

Let's look at this from a different perspective. Forget everything you just read about the Triangle and Square Funds. Instead, imagine buying one share of ABC stock at $10. One month later, the stock is worth $5. You just lost half your money. In order to get your money back, you need to wait for the stock price to increase to $10 per share. Unless you decide to buy another share of ABC stock at $5, your total investment at this point is $15. You bought one share at $10 and another share at $5.

At what share price do you break even?

You break even at $7.50 per share. At $7.50 per share, your two shares are worth $15. This is the same as your total investment. You will make money at anything above $7.50. At $8 per share, you have $16. At $9 per share, you have $18 and, by the time ABC stock regains the original

$10 price when you bought your first share, you now have $20. This is $5 more than you invested.

By purchasing the second share at $5, you reduced your average from $10 (you only had one share) to $7.50 (you had two shares). You bought a share at $10 and you bought a share at $5. Your average price per share is $7.50. Instead of price, think of it as your *cost*. Buying a second share at a reduced *cost* lowered your *average cost*. Hence the phrase, *dollar cost averaging*.[2]

Every time you buy an additional share, it changes your overall cost per share, which changes your overall *average* share price. The average price becomes your breakeven share price. You are making money at any price above the average.

If an investment goes down in value, you can dollar cost average into the investment with additional money. This allows your potential profit to happen sooner as the investment recovers.

In 2006, Mary opened college savings plans for her three grandchildren. They were young and she wanted to be aggressive with the money. She knew to expect some ups and downs along the way. She contributed $2,500 to each of the accounts in each of the first three years. During this time frame, we were experiencing a downturn in the economy. As of February 2009, the $7,500 she invested in each account was worth about $5,000.

---

[2] Dollar cost averaging does not ensure a profit and does not protect against loss in declining markets. Since dollar cost averaging involves continuous investment in securities regardless of fluctuating price levels of such securities, the investor should consider his financial ability to continue his purchases through periods of low price levels.

Mary had no way of knowing this bear market was coming to an end and we were about to enter into one of the strongest and longest bull markets in the history of the stock market. At this point, she contributed another $5,000 to each of the three accounts. She understood the concept of buying more when the investments are cheap. Mary's decision will have a huge impact on her grandchildren's future. The significant growth she realized on her contributions while the markets were low will go a very long way toward paying for their college tuition when the time comes.

This same concept is vital to retirement planning, as well. It is not always about finding consistent and steady performers. Sometimes, especially when adding money on a regular basis to an account, you want some volatility. It can actually give your overall return a boost.

When you retire, you no longer contribute to your retirement account. So, how can you dollar cost average?

This is an excellent question and the answer can be found in the following pages.

Chapter 8

THE BUCKET SYSTEM
OUR CORE STRATEGY

Time to crack open your nest egg!

Before you crack open the nest egg, it's important to remember you only get one chance to do it right. There are no second chances. You only retire once and there is no practice. If you make a mistake, you likely won't know you made a mistake until ten or 15 years down the road. Then, it's too late to fix. A mistake can be made if you choose the wrong investments, take too much monthly income, or let your emotions overwhelm rational thinking.

So far in this book, you've learned about many of the common fears and concerns retirees face before transitioning from work to retirement life. We've discussed emotions and the impact they have on your decision making, especially when it comes to money. You've also become knowledgeable about some very important concepts: time horizon (as it pertains to a retiree), sequence of returns, and dollar cost averaging. These concepts ultimately form the foundation and reasoning behind the strategy[3] you are about to learn.

It's time to grab the eggs, frying pan, and spatula. You are going to learn how to crack open and cook the perfect nest egg!

Many retirees think of their nest egg as one lump sum of money. It may not be all in one account. Perhaps some of it is in a 401(k), other parts in a Roth IRA, a spouse's 403(b), a Traditional IRA, etc. No matter where it is or how many accounts it is spread among, most people view their nest egg as one cumulative lump sum of money they have set aside for retirement. And, they tend to manage it the same way across the board.

There are some very fundamental pitfalls and challenges with managing and thinking about your money in this manner. To examine these challenges, let's first think of ourselves as having a $1,000,000 nest egg. This is a nice round number so the math is easy. The strategy you are about to learn can be implemented with $50,000 or $5 million. The dollar amount is completely irrelevant to the strategy.

To go along with your $1,000,000 nest egg, there is social security income and possibly a pension, depending on where you worked. These income sources are not enough to enjoy the lifestyle you wish to live during retirement. As a result, you decide to withdraw a 4% income stream from your nest egg every year ($40,000 per year).

---

[3] All investing involves risk, including the potential loss of principal, and there can be no guarantee that any investment strategy will be successful.

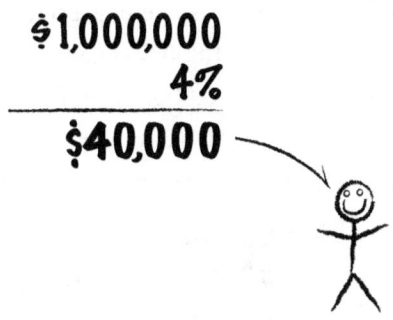

A 4% to 5% withdrawal stream from a nest egg is the general rule of thumb many financial advisors use when determining a suitable and sustainable income stream during retirement. If the retiree is older, the income stream can be a bit higher. If younger, the income stream should be a little lower. Either way, for our example, we are taking a 4% income stream from your nest egg.

Since you are retired, you want to be fairly conservative with the asset allocation for your nest egg. At this stage of the game, you can't tolerate any fluctuations in your accounts. After all, what you have is what you have.

Just like during your working years, unexpected things happen. You may need to come up with money to replace a furnace, remodel a bathroom, help your children or grandchildren, buy a new car, or cover unexpected medical expenses. No matter the reason, there will always be unexpected expenses that come up and trigger the need for additional cash above and beyond your monthly income during retirement.

Go back to the illustration depicting the 4% income stream from your $1,000,000 nest egg. Imagine you need to come up with $50,000 for some unexpected expense. You take $50,000 from your $1,000,000 nest egg, bringing your relative value down to $950,000. Now you are taking a 4% income stream from $950,000. You just gave yourself a pay cut in retirement! This is the last thing you want to do.

The money lumped together as a single nest egg managed the same way across the board can allow for a reasonable income stream during retirement. But, it does not allow much freedom when it comes to the need for additional cash.

Investing in the same moderately conservative manner can also leave very little flexibility during your retirement life. Inflation, over a 20- or 30-year retirement, can do some damage to the buying power of your incomes streams if you are too conservative with too much of your nest egg in your earlier retirement years.

In order to address these challenges, let's divide your nest egg into two buckets: a Growth Bucket and an Income Bucket.[4] As you would expect, the Income Bucket

---

[4] This illustration does not reflect any particular investment and does not project future results. It is simply an illustration of dividing money into two different investment buckets and illustrates compound growth over time.

represents the bucket of money to draw an income stream from during retirement. The Growth Bucket represents the money set aside to let grow.[5]

How much goes in the Income Bucket depends on how much income you need from your nest egg. The remaining money goes into the Growth Bucket. Let's assume you place 75% of your $1 million nest egg into the Income Bucket and the remaining money into the Growth Bucket. You will then draw an income stream from the $750,000 Income Bucket to supplement your other income sources in retirement.

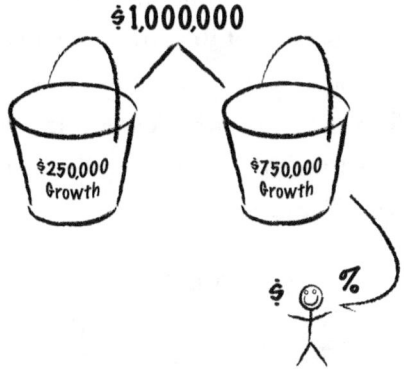

The income drawn from the Income Bucket is very important to you. It is how you pay your bills and maintain your lifestyle. Because of this, the Income Bucket itself and how it's managed are also very important to you.

Since you rely on income from the Income Bucket to live your life, it is recommended to invest this money into

---

[5] Please remember investing involves risks, and the value of your investment will fluctuate over time and you may gain or lose money.

a moderately conservative asset allocation. On a scale of one to ten, with ten being very aggressive and one being ultra safe, the Income Bucket is best allocated as a three or four on this scale, depending on how old you are when you retire.

The Growth Bucket, on the other hand, is out of sight, out of mind. Yes, it is still important to you but what the account is worth from day to day, month to month, or year to year has minimal impact on how you live your life. Your Growth Bucket and your income stream have very little to do with each other. What happens in the Growth Bucket has very little bearing on anything in the short term. Because of this, you should be willing to accept a little more fluctuation from the asset allocation you select for your Growth Bucket. On the same one to ten scale, the Growth Bucket is best allocated as a six or seven (moderately aggressive).

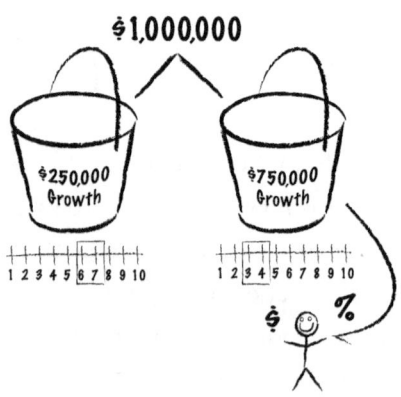

Dividing your nest egg in this manner accomplishes several very significant things.

When an unexpected expense arises, such as an emergency or something fun you want to do, you simply pull that money from your Growth Bucket. When you withdraw from your Growth Bucket, it has no impact on your Income Bucket. Therefore, your income stream is not affected in any manner. This strategy allows you to keep pace with inflation over the long term. Let's assume the Growth Bucket increases from $250,000 to $300,000 over a certain period of time. Depending on the economy, this could take less than a year or several years. Regardless of how long it takes for the growth to happen, the $50,000 gain is moved from the Growth Bucket into the Income Bucket.

By moving the gains from Growth to Income, you effectively accomplish two very important things. First, you give yourself a raise. Shifting the gains to the Income Bucket makes the Income Bucket larger, which increases the income power of that portion of the nest egg. This gives you a higher income stream. In other words, it gives you a raise and allows you to keep pace with inflation. The gains from the Growth Bucket feed the Income Bucket, which feeds your bottom line over time.

The second thing you accomplish by shifting gains from the Growth side to the Income side is that you protect the gains as you go. In essence, you are moving the gains from the more aggressive bucket to the more conservative bucket.

The capacity to give yourself a raise AND protect your gains simply by moving the gains from one bucket to another is a very key part of what makes The Bucket System, our core strategy, so powerful.

We are just getting started with this strategy in terms of what it will accomplish for you in retirement. There are three points to keep in mind:

1) You have a place to go for money without affecting your income stream in retirement (unexpected expenses come from the Growth Bucket).
2) Your income increases over time as you use the gains from the Growth Bucket to feed the Income Bucket (this feeds the bottom line).
3) By moving your gains from the more aggressive bucket to the more conservative bucket, they are protected.

Now let's circle back to the three core concepts you learned earlier in this book (time horizon, sequence of return, and dollar cost averaging) and see how they relate to the Growth and Income Bucket strategy.

As you recall, many retirees think of their nest egg as one lump sum of money managed in the same way (conservative). From the Time Horizon chapter, you learned retirement is really a series of staggered time horizons. Some of the money in your nest egg will be spent shortly after you retire. But, most of it will not be touched for 10, 20, or 30-plus years. Your ten-year money should not be managed the same way as your 30-year money.

The Growth and Income Bucket strategy will naturally stagger your time horizons. The Income Bucket is moderately conservative. Having 50% to 75% of your nest egg in the Income Bucket allows plenty of "leftover" money to fund the Growth Bucket. The Growth Bucket is more aggressive and grants you the opportunity to keep pace with inflation over time. If all your money were as moderately conservative as the Income Bucket, inflation and taxes will likely overwhelm you down the road. With a moderately aggressive Growth Bucket, it's a nice opportunity to keep pace with inflation because you use the gains from the Growth Bucket to feed the Income Bucket.

The second concept we will circle back to is sequence of returns. When you are accumulating money for retirement, the sequence of returns does not matter; only the average matters. When you are in the distribution phase and withdrawing income from your nest egg, sequence of returns matters a lot. In fact, the sequence of returns can make or break the entire outcome of your nest egg. While in the distribution phase, the sequence of returns is far more important than the average return you earn on your money.

The Bucket System addresses the sequence of returns concept quite nicely. The Income Bucket is in the distribution phase. In this bucket, sequence of returns matter. It is critical to limit your fluctuation in the Income Bucket and accept a slightly lower long-run return. With the Income Bucket invested moderately conservatively, this works out well.

The Growth Bucket is on the other side of the equation. Even though you are retired, you are not taking income from the Growth Bucket. Because of this, it is technically still in the accumulation phase. Money is set aside to grow for the future. It is no different than what you were doing during your working years. Because you are not taking income from the Growth Bucket, the fluctuation in the account does not matter. The sequence of returns does not matter. The average return is what counts. In a more aggressive portfolio, over a longer period of time, you should achieve a higher rate of return. These higher returns give you the power to combat inflation.

Dollar cost averaging is next. A fluctuating investment, when added to regularly, may have the potential to achieve a higher return than a portfolio that grows consistently every year. The key component is **adding to it on a regular basis**. So, how can dollar cost averaging come into play when you are no longer working and not adding regularly to a retirement account?

With The Bucket System, dollar cost averaging occurs within the Growth Bucket. In this bucket, as dividends and capital gains are earned, they will be reinvested. A moderately aggressive, healthy dividend-paying asset allocation is part of a well-rounded Growth Bucket. Allowing the dividends in your Growth Bucket to reinvest is almost as good as contributing to the account yourself.

The good thing about reinvesting dividends inside the Growth Bucket is that the Growth Bucket is the more aggressive one. Therefore, it will have the most fluctuation. Fluctuation is exactly what you want with dollar cost averaging or, in this case, reinvesting your dividends. The Growth and Income Bucket strategy sets you up very nicely for this.

Before we go further, let's take a moment to review. Growth and Income Buckets allow you to keep pace with inflation by using the gains from the Growth Bucket to feed the Income Bucket. This feeds the bottom line. In doing so, it allows you to protect the gains by moving them from the more aggressive bucket to the more conservative bucket. It is a place to obtain money (Growth Bucket) for large expenses without reducing your income stream. You also learned how the strategy addresses the challenge of managing your time horizon during retirement, as well as sequence of return risk—all the while, giving you the ability to take advantage of dollar cost averaging.

Now you will learn how the strategy addresses the emotions and common fears many retirees have during retirement.

The First Common Fear Is: "Will I Run Out of Money?"

You certainly do not want to outlive your money. You want your money to last as long as you do. Let's see how the Growth and Income Bucket strategy addresses this concern. Ultimately, your income stream is perpetually enhanced by using the gains from the Growth Bucket to feed the Income Bucket. The goal is not only to preserve the income, but to grow the income over time.

The Second Common Fear Is: "Am I Maximizing My Potential?"

As mentioned earlier, it would be a shame to work somewhere for 20, 30, or 40 years, save diligently for retirement, and then not realize everything out of retirement you want to.

Julie retired after 47 years of employment. She always dreamed of taking her grandkids to Disney World. With five grandkids, two daughters, and two sons-in-law, she knew it would be an expensive trip. She retired in August 2008, just before the major market decline that occurred during the fall of 2008. Timing could not have been worse.

Her Income Bucket and Growth Bucket were established. She started with $250,000 in her Growth Bucket and the rest of her nest egg was positioned in her Income Bucket. She took a monthly income stream from her Income Bucket to supplement Social Security.

When the major market crash occurred in the following months, her Growth Bucket, being moderately aggressive, declined in value. The Income Bucket, positioned much more conservatively, experienced only modest downward pressure.

She was not worried about finances because the Growth Bucket had nothing to do with her income stream. It had no bearing on her standard of living. By the end of 2011, not only did her Growth Bucket fully recover, she actually had a $50,000 gain to show for staying the course. (A key component of the Bucket System is to use the gains from the Growth Bucket to feed the Income Bucket. However, that does not mean you need to move ALL the gains.)

Julie had her heart set on taking her family to Disney World. She moved $40,000 of gains from Growth to Income and used the additional $10,000 gain to take her family to Disney World. Now that's maximizing retirement!

Take a moment to put this into perspective. In this scenario, not only did Julie gain $50,000 in the Growth Bucket, she gave herself a raise by moving $40,000 of that gain to the Income Bucket. The other $10,000 is put toward a family trip to Disney World. The $40,000 gain is now protected because she moved it from the more aggressive bucket to the more conservative bucket. This is just one example of the power of the Growth and Income Bucket strategy.

The Third Common Fear the Strategy Addresses Is: "I Don't Want to Be So Worried about My Financial Life that I Can't Enjoy My Retirement Life."

This fear is centered around the emotional power of money. It is very common to worry about your money. You don't want to run out and you don't want to lose it.

After all, you may feel the pain of losing it is twice as high as the joy of earning the same amount.

Dividing the nest egg into Growth and Income Buckets makes managing your emotions much easier. Because the Growth Bucket is invested more aggressively than the Income Bucket, it is going to fluctuate more. As you know, the Growth Bucket has very little to do with your standard of living. Keeping the Growth Bucket separate from your lifestyle-sustaining Income Bucket goes a very long way toward managing your emotions in retirement. You are not concerned about the short-term volatility of the Growth Bucket because it has no bearing on your income.

Refer to our Disney World story. Assume you took $10,000 to pay for the trip and protected your $40,000 gain by moving it to your Income Bucket. Then, suddenly, the markets declined. The Growth Bucket is more aggressive so you would assume the Growth Bucket declined in value as well. Let's assume it fell in value from $250,000 to $230,000. Does that get your attention? **Yes**. But, are you worried about it? **No**. You have the money you need for Disney World, protected the $40,000 of gains, AND gave yourself a raise. Life is good. So, you sit tight, enjoy your retirement, and wait for the growth bucket to recover before repeating the process. You can see how the emotional swings of the economy and the markets can have very little, if any, impact on the way you live your life in retirement.

We have one other point to discuss with regard to the Growth and Income Bucket strategy. Do you remember who said, "Be greedy when others are fearful and be fearful when others are greedy."? That's right. Warren Buffet. Growth and Income Buckets tie into this concept very well. Markets tend to cycle. Over time, they generally rise, but along the way there are some ups and downs. By dividing your money into the two buckets, you will control your emotions and insulate your income stream from the market's ups and downs.

The moral of the story is to buy low and sell high. How do you know when things are low? When everyone is fearful and everyone wants out. How do you know when things are high? When everyone is greedy and everyone wants in.

When everyone wants in, prices rise and the markets rise. The greater the rise and the faster the rise, the greater the risk of a correction as markets retract to more reasonable levels. This is why moving your gains from the Growth Bucket to the Income Bucket is so crucial. By moving your gains from Growth to Income, you are essentially selling high. This is exactly what you want to do. You are taking gains as prices rise. If prices go down, no worries, you just protected your gains.

When the markets are performing very well for an extended period of time, often the opportunity arises to move gains from Growth to Income several times. Looking at our example again, your Growth Bucket may increase from $250,000 to $300,000. You move the $50,000 gain to the Income side. This resets the Growth Bucket to $250,000. A short time down the road, it is back to $300,000. So, you move the gains again.

At this point, the questions are: "Why shift the $50,000 gain to the Income Bucket when things are going well? Shouldn't that money stay invested the way it is?" These questions point to greed. And that's when you need to be fearful, because that's when corrections happen. At the end of the day, no one has ever gone broke making a profit. If you move a $50,000 gain from Growth to Income and the markets continue to rally, your strategy works! You still have $250,000 working for you. If the markets retract, you will be happy you moved your gains and gave yourself a raise in the process.

The Growth and Income Bucket strategy overcomes many different challenges faced as a retiree when it comes to managing your nest egg. To sum up:

1) It allows you to keep pace with inflation.
2) Protects your gains as you go.
3) Staggers your time horizons.
4) Overcomes sequence of return risk.
5) Takes advantage of dollar cost averaging.
6) Helps ensure you will not run out of money.
7) Helps maximize your potential.
8) Allows you to control your emotions.

This strategy should be the cornerstone of your financial plan when determining how to structure your nest egg in retirement.

Chapter 9

COOKING THE EGG

*The egg has been cracked.
No pieces of shell anywhere. Now what?*

Now that you know how to crack the nest egg open, it is time to learn how to cook the egg. So far, you have been exposed to and understand several key concepts behind the core Growth and Income Bucket Strategy. You have learned the importance of dividing your nest egg into two different buckets, Growth and Income. In this section, we will break down the types of investments to use in each of these buckets.

It is important to note each bucket is not limited to only one account. In fact, both your income bucket and your growth bucket should be comprised of several different accounts. It is common to have two, three, or even four accounts in each bucket. There are several reasons for this. First, it is necessary to have enough accounts to accommodate the various account registrations (Traditional IRA, Roth IRA, Individual, Joint, Trust, Non-Qualified, Qualified, etc.) you may have. Second, if you are married, your spouse likely has some retirement assets as well, and that will require additional accounts. Third, different types of investments will be used at different periods and for different reasons. It's possible to have a brokerage account, an annuity, and a certificate of deposit all used for different reasons. Again, this increases the need for multiple accounts within each of your buckets.

Cooking with Traditional and Roth IRAs

Let's first examine how to incorporate Traditional IRA and Roth IRA money into your bucket strategy. As you learned in the previous chapter, your Income Bucket is used to generate an income stream to supplement your other cash flow sources in retirement. Since your Income Bucket should produce a predictable stream of income every year, you will go into every year knowing what your taxable income will be. Therefore, you will know how much tax to withhold on your IRA distributions for that year. Knowing your Social Security income, any pension income, and income from your Income Bucket will tell you what your tax liability will be for the year.

Since most distributions from Traditional IRAs[6] are taxable, the Income Bucket makes a great parking place for a large portion of your Traditional IRA during retirement. With that in mind, you learned it is imperative to use the gains from the Growth Bucket to feed the Income Bucket, which feeds the income stream. In order to effectively

---

[6] Please remember investing involves risks, and the value of your investment will fluctuate over time and you may gain or lose money.

accomplish this, Traditional IRA money should be in the Growth Bucket, as well.

This is absolutely vital to the overall strategy. In order to move money from one account to another, money needs to move from "like to like" registrations (from Traditional IRA to Traditional IRA). When moving money from one bucket to another, you are moving money from one account to another. In order to move from "like to like" accounts, you need a Traditional IRA in both the Growth Bucket and Income Bucket. This gives you an account to move money from and an account to receive money that both have the same registration—in this case, Traditional IRAs.

Roth IRAs, on the other hand, are a completely different animal. As you know, the tax advantages of a Roth IRA are far superior to the tax advantages of a Traditional IRA. The biggest advantage the Roth IRA has over the Traditional IRA is the fact that distributions from a Roth IRA are generally not taxable. With this in mind, Roth IRAs are an ideal candidate for the Growth Bucket.

The Growth Bucket serves several purposes. One of those is to give you a place to obtain money without affecting your income stream. The Growth Bucket is tapped into for large ticket purchases like cars, home improvement, travel, etc. With the Roth IRA positioned in the Growth Bucket, it provides a great place to withdraw money from for such purposes because it does not affect your tax bracket for the year!

Roth IRAs are a bit newer than Traditional IRAs, so most people have a relatively small amount of their nest egg allocated to Roth IRAs. Most nest eggs are in the form of a Traditional IRA, 401(k), and 403(b), etc. As a result, placing the entire Roth account(s) in the Growth Bucket with the Traditional IRA money split between Growth and Income buckets works out very well.

The Income Bucket—Key Ingredients

When creating a predictable and sustainable income stream for yourself in retirement, it is critical to design the Income Bucket to allow your income stream to generate a consistent rate regardless of how investments in the account perform.

Dividends and interest are two great examples of how this is accomplished. Dividends are an extremely powerful income-producing component of your Income Bucket. When structured appropriately, a dividend stream and your account value have very little to do with each other. The key phrase is "when structured appropriately."

Some stocks, ETFs (Exchange Traded Funds), or Mutual Funds will pay a dividend for owning shares of the stock or fund. A dividend is simply a company sharing its profits with you. This usually happens on a quarterly basis. If you buy a share of stock, sometimes that stock will pay you a certain dollar amount every quarter while you own the stock.

To further examine the income power of dividends, let's looks at a real world example: AT&T. As one of our country's largest telecommunications company's,

AT&T pays a very attractive dividend every year to its shareholders. We are not endorsing or condoning investing in AT&T. This is merely an example to illustrate the power of owning investments like AT&T in your Income Bucket.

When a company pays a dividend to a shareholder, it is essentially sharing its profits with the shareholder. A shareholder owns a piece of the company and, as a result, gets to share in the profits of the company in the form of a dividend. Not every company pays a dividend because some companies decide to reinvest 100% of their earnings (profits) back into the company to continue to grow. Others, like AT&T, choose to pay a dividend to investors.

As of May 27, 2014, AT&T was trading at $35.21 per share. Also, as of this date, their annual dividend was declared at $1.84 per share. This is, of course, an annualized dividend. The actual quarterly payout would be 46 cents per share ($1.84/4 quarters). This means, as a shareholder, every quarter AT&T will pay you 46 cents for every share of AT&T you own. With a $1.84 per share annualized dividend and a $35.21 share price, AT&T is yielding 5.23% ($1.84/$35.21).

As you can see, it's a very attractive dividend stream. This type of investment is especially well suited for the Income Bucket.

As mentioned earlier, one of the key goals when constructing an Income Bucket is to create an income stream that is unaffected by fluctuations in the account. An investment such as AT&T fits the bill nicely because it is what's known as a "dividend aristocrat." Only about 50 companies in the entire stock market carry this prestigious title. Dividend aristocrats have increased their dividend payout to investors every year for at least 25 consecutive years. This means every year a shareholder continued to own AT&T, the shareholder continued to be paid more and more to own it. Every year, like clockwork, the dividend per share has increased.

In fact, since 1985, AT&T's dividend has increased over 900%.[7] Now that's how to keep pace with inflation!

Taking it a step further, as the Growth Bucket increases in value, the gains are moved to the Income Bucket. When this takes place, you buy more shares of what you own in the Income Bucket. When more shares of a dividend aristocrat are bought, you are buying a higher income stream. You are giving yourself a raise! When dividends are paid per share and the gains from the Growth Bucket are used to buy more shares of the investments in the Income Bucket, a raise is given regardless of the performance of the underlying holdings at the time. Buying more shares buys more income because now you own more shares that pay more dividends.

Owning individual stocks in your nest egg may or may not be suitable for you. AT&T is only used as an example because it is the type of investment that may be part of an Income Bucket. It is easier to discuss dividends

---

[7] Past performance is not indicative of future results.

in relation to an individual stock rather than in relation to an ETF or Mutual Fund.

It is also very important to understand that not all stocks, mutual funds, and ETFs are created equal. Not all dividend aristocrats are created equal, either.

When it comes to the Income Bucket, it is imperative to be extremely selective about choosing investments. A good investment for the Income Bucket is what we call "recession resistant" sectors. These sectors include consumer foods, consumer staples, energy, utilities, pharmaceuticals, and telecommunications. Regardless of the state of the economy, people still pay their electric bill and take their prescription drugs. Investing in these six sectors in a very specific and deliberate manner services the Income Bucket well in both good and bad market conditions. What is a sector and should it be explained here.

Beyond dividend-paying stocks, mutual funds, and ETFs, the Income Bucket may also consist of bond funds, certificates of deposit (CDs), fixed annuities,[8] or variable annuities. Many different factors go into deciding when and how to implement these types of investments into the Income Bucket. The interest rate environment at the time, along with income goals, goes a long way toward determining which of these types of investments are suitable for your situation.

---

8 Guarantees from insurance companies are based on the claims-paying ability of the issuing insurance company.

The Growth Bucket—A Chicken that Keeps Laying Fresh Eggs

Because the Growth Bucket is the more aggressive bucket, it is invested much differently than the Income Bucket. It's important to invest in a healthy and consistently increasing dividend stream, but you will broaden your investment exposure in your Growth Bucket across additional sectors and geographic regions, when compared to the Income Bucket. While the Income Bucket should focus on consumer food, consumer staples, energy, utilities, telecommunications, and pharmaceuticals, the Growth Bucket will incorporate real estate, financials, industrial, and technology as well. Here again, it may make sense to favor the attractive dividend-paying equities in these sectors. It's significant to take advantage of the dollar cost averaging concept by consistently buying more and more shares at various prices through dividend reinvestment.

Beyond dividend-paying equities, the Growth Bucket will also house your international investments, from both emerging markets and established markets. It will serve as a parking place for your small and mid-cap investments.

The ingredients used when cooking the nest egg are just as relevant as how you crack it open. There is a lot of planning, thought, and experience needed to create the perfect nest egg. This section was designed to give you some insight into the thought process behind the types of investments that make up the ingredients within the two buckets.

Chapter 10

THE NEXT STEP

Plan to achieve your desired goals

When it comes to retirement planning, one of the best things you can do for yourself is to sit down and put together a plan. The plan should take into account your goals, needs, and wants. It should factor in your desired lifestyle, life expectancy, inflation projections, return projections, income stream projections, tax brackets, etc.

The concept of Growth and Income Buckets is not a template. It is a foundation. There is no one-size-fits-all ratio between Growth and Income. Some people need 20% of their nest egg in the Income Bucket while others need 90% of their nest egg allocated toward their Income Bucket. Everyone's situation is different. A plan will utilize the necessary information needed to determine how much income needs to be generated for someone. That will guide how much of the nest egg goes into the Income Bucket.

After a plan is compete, it needs to be implemented. Once implemented, it should be monitored and maintained. Adjustments should be made, if necessary, to ensure staying on track toward the goals.

It does not matter if you are retired, soon to be retired, or a long way from retirement. It does not matter if you have a lot of money or are just starting out. Either way, a financial plan is needed and should be monitored on a regular basis.

The Growth and Income Bucket System is a phenomenal strategy that can easily be incorporated into anyone's retirement plan. It is a common sense, practical strategy that has helped many people transition into retirement with clarity and confidence about their future. When implemented correctly and monitored regularly, it will change the way you live your life in retirement.

It is never too early or too late to start planning. No matter your stage in life, it's important to make sure you are on the right path. You won't even know the path you are on unless you sit down and crunch some numbers. Planning isn't easy, but it is a critical part of achieving your desired goals. Now you know what you are building toward and how to structure your nest egg. One day it will be time for you to crack open your nest egg—*Sunny Side Up!*[9]

---

[9] www.mysunnysideup.com is available as a resource to gain a deeper understanding of the different retirement planning concepts discussed in this book.

AFTERWORD

The Tranel Financial Group was founded in 1988. We have worked hard to deliver practical strategies and innovative tools to help our clients reach the financial milestones in their lives that are most important to them.

Our clients often tell us how they wish they knew then what they know now. We hear over and over from clients that they wish they would have learned more about investing and approached their savings differently when they were younger, so they could benefit from that knowledge now that they are older.

The goal of this book is to educate you on several important retirement planning concepts and ultimately weave those concepts together into our firm's core retirement planning strategy—The Bucket System.

The world can be unpredictable, but your retirement planning doesn't have to be. This proven strategy helps deliver peace of mind in good markets and in bad. It helps ensure you are prepared and protected no matter what the future may bring.

Knowledge and understanding of this strategy is the first step. Implementing the strategy and customizing the strategy around your specific needs is the next step. We can't emphasize enough how important it is to work with a team of professionals when it comes to structuring your own personal Bucket System strategy.

Our dedicated team of Financial Advisors are committed to one simple goal: delivering real and measurable results. We will keep working to deliver financial independence and peace of mind to everyone we serve.

Visit our website today at **www.mysunnysideup.com** for additional information and to sign up for:

- Complimentary Discovery Meeting with a Tranel Financial Group Advisor
- Complimentary **Sunny Side Up** Seminar
- Complimentary **Sunny Side Up** E-Book

We look forward to meeting with you to show you just how you can crack open the perfect nest egg to *Enjoy A Better Life*™.

The Sunny Side Up Team at The Tranel Financial Group
1509 N. Milwaukee Ave., Libertyville, Illinois 60048
847.680.9052

ABOUT THE AUTHORS

ROCH TRANEL, Certified Financial Planner, is CEO and founder of The Tranel Financial Group located in Libertyville, Illinois. Roch has been helping individuals reach clarity and confidence about their financial future for over 25 years. Helping people *Enjoy A Better Life*™ through successful financial planning is Roch's passion in life. Roch has assembled a team of professional financial advisors who are committed to the same principles and share the same commitment to providing an unparalleled client experience.

As an active leader in his community, Roch has served on several boards, including the GLMV Chamber, The Rotary Club, and Great Lakes Adaptive Sports Association. Roch is also very passionate and active in growing The Tranel Movement, which includes leadership, community growth, and networking opportunities.

Roch resides in Libertyville, Illinois, with his wife, Kathleen, and their children, Jenna and Alec.

BENJAMIN PAHL is a Financial Advisor and Director of Financial Institutions at The Tranel Financial Group in Libertyville, Illinois. Since 2005, Ben has worked to help hundreds of clients with their retirement planning and investment management. Ben specializes in helping people make difficult life transition decisions.

Passionate about helping others, Ben has an ability to assess a client's complex situation, simplify it, and put together an actionable game plan that will allow his clients to reach their financial goals. In his day-to-day role at The Tranel Financial Group, Ben is responsible for actively implementing the concepts and strategies laid out in this book—putting them to use with real world clients and situations.

Ben resides in Salem, Wisconsin with his wife, Nicole, and children Brady and Madalynn.